THE FORLORN ENCHANTRESS
Verses Distilled in Love

Isha Maheshwari

**All India Forum for English Students
Scholars and Trainers (AIFEST)**

The Forlorn Enchantress: Verses Distilled in Love
Isha Maheshwari

First Published: April 2021

All India Forum for English Students Scholars and Trainers (AIFEST)

Amazon KDP ISBN: 9798737045661

Editing and Proofreading

Prof Manu Mangattu
Mob: 9496322323

Cover Design

Mr Bijeeshkumar Shaji
Mob: 9745390453

To

Lado, My Sweet Princess

My Parents and Members of My Family
&
The Nameless Gypsy who Inspired these Verses

* * * * *

Contents

1
A Gypsy in Love

I am a wanderer in love,
I am wandering as a gypsy,
Searching for love in its most diamond form.
The quest continues,
Stopping in the dark lanes,
Waiting in the silent greens,
With conscientious introspections,
For it is a feeling of rare possibilities.
For, it holds more of lust,
And less of its true nature.
Lacking in permanence, for it is difficult to hold.
The search continues until it pauses,
For a soothing calm feeling,
Of the highest of all emotions- love.

2
All Shades of Romance

How would it be my love
To feel all shades of romance?
We walking past the morning sun,
In the dry coastal sand.
Holding hand in hand we walk so far,
Forgetting the range of lands.
My love I seek to be lost in your world,
To feel your caring hands.
I feel each day should start this way.
Along the coastal sand.

We ride together the mountain heights,
Me hiding in your arms.
The warmth and love you make me feel,
Those joys hold no bounds.
Two bodies apart but souls being one,
The joys and pains shared together,
Should be observed by us but none.

That love is the best that holds respect,
For individuality and personal choice.
No one forcing the other,
To think the way they want.
Then flows the love that spreads around,
Like a prism of light,
Converging the seven into one.

3
The Rhetorical Question

I love you so much but don't ask me why.
I admire you so much but don't make me admit that.
I feel your presence but don't let me accept that.
Still all my thoughts reach you,
I know you know that.

Let the days pass by,
Let the months, let the years pass by,
With it let the silent language of love pass by
Just like the passing by of a cool breeze
And with it the aroma of freshly grown roses.

Let me love you not for a day or two, but till eternity.
Let me love you so but don't ask me why.

4
Hide and Seek

You left me in the forests, dense and green,
I became one with snarling wild beasts.
You pushed me into the depths of the ocean,
I emerged as a shark with sharp tearing teeth.
You forced me into the roaring flames,
I turned into pure yellow gold shedding all that was impure.
You jerked me from the edge of a high raised wall,
I perched down proud with an eagle sweep.
You pricked thorns on me, big and small,
Bled me with every pierce.
You tried your trials, I rehearsed my rehearsals.
You failed, I emerged victorious.

A hunter with a net were you,
I, a bird with flapping wings.
My soft low prayers reached heaven after long tiring queues,
Since God was busy listening to the earth's shrieking cries.
The unheard answers flung into action.
The victim no longer feels victimized.
This knowledge satiates and saturates me,
As I continue life's hide and seek.

5
It's Time You Leave for Your New Found Love

I still remember the day,
You came close to me and closer still,
Trying to feel the natural odour of me,
Wanting to tell me that you were in love with me,
Not knowing that I knew that still.

Moments added up to hours,
Hours added up to days,
You continued to express your love,
Waiting until that one day I'd say,
'Yes', I too was in love.
Days passed by in work,
Nights passed by in silence.

Then one day I saw you with a new found love,
The pain of which I could not bear,
To see my love as someone else's love,
But I could bear the fickleness of the human mind,
That looks for pleasures.
And to me it became clearer still,
It is a world not of emotions but of lust,
And I became happy to see you happy,
With your new found love.

6
Let Me Glow in Your Love

For me it continues to be a puzzle
Why you came into my life like the small rainy months
Soothing me like a gush of cold water,
Calming me like a cloud freed from the skies?

Tell me love what I should do now,
When I know it can't last any longer?
Tell me love what can I do now,
When I know it can't grow any longer?
Tell me love before receding away from me,
Don't leave me love with a suffocating me.

My love I'll keep you as a treasure,
As the most valued possession.
I'll store your love as God's gift to me,
As the rarest of all possessions.
I will keep your love as a beautiful memory,
In some recesses of my mind.
Whenever you see me glow in love,
It is for you that I shine.

7
Look Back My Love

How do I desist myself my love?
How to stop myself from the truth?
My moments I pass brooding of you,
Silently admiring the you in you.
Me sitting eye to eye with you,
To be lost in your world.
To be dragged by none who is my own.

You speaking in your silence,
Me entangled in your charms.
You smiling in happiness,
Me happy with those smiles,
You voicing your mortal desires,
I, feeling heavenly in your nearness.
You exploring your ideas,
Me, a silent listener.
You having finished conversing,
I seek reasons to stop you from stopping.

My eyes meet your eyes again,
Your parting look give a prickly pain.
Mind said stop, mouth stood mute.
Heart became heavy, don't part my love.
Eyes overflowing with tears.
The red eyes gave you a shivering pain,
As stood you by the door.
Came running back in my hug.
Grasping me tight like an iron pulling a magnet,
A soothing blend of joy and pain.
'Don't let your tears turn me dry,
I'll be back my love, never to let you cry'.

8
Love Infinite

You are the bee, I am the rose.
You suck me, I feel the essence of your love.
You are the wanderer, I am the lurer.
You are in search of fragrance,
I hold it, I release it.
You circle around me, I am the beautiest of all.
Let's grow together, let's wither together,
Me, my red petals, you your colourless wings.
Let's live together, let's die together,
Making our love sublime.

9
Love Reveals its Language

'My love, why are you being so silent?'
I asked the growing love within me.
She blushed like a red winter rose and said,
'No choice as the one who shall feel it
Is like me too, silent and intense.'
She said, 'I exist in the calm understanding
Between the moving clouds and the still sky'.
'I am there in the hushed whispers
Between the rhythmic gushing waterfalls and the intact hills'.
'I am the poem between the rustling green leaves
And the rough brown shapeless tree trunks'.
'So diverse but existing in unison, that's my definition.'
'I have no limits, no horizon,
The more I'm explored, the more mysterious I become.'
'The deeper you dive the more intense I become.'

So the human lives of impermanence
Get deeply delved into the permanence of love.
Again contrasting ideas juxtaposed,
To create miracles out of the mysterious,
Causing human lives to breathe their mortal breath,
Leaving behind the immortal love to breathe on and on and
on.
The weaker clutching the stronger strongly in her arms.
That's the power of mortality over immortality
That's that reality of mortality and love,
Love being a meek gentle animal,
Before the human undefined.

10
Love Undefined

My whole being is in search of a love.

The love that goes deep down the senses,
The love that satisfies not only the body but also the being.

The love, thinking of which I lose myself into happiness,
The love, the thought of which fills me with shyness.

The love which needs no questioning of space and free will,
The love which evokes no fear and no jealousy,
The love which reaches its zenith of infinity.

Is there a lover who share similar matches?

11
Muted Love

Is our love mute?
Does it need a voice?
Only to be felt when needed? Otherwise not?
Has our love no right,
To bloom like the colourful winter flowers?
Is it meant to be like the voiceless expression
Of the unheard characters of a play?
Or is it just one sided?
With me just hearing the echoes of the love I cry out?
Crushing me under the impression that
It's the reciprocating love.

There's faith flowing in from one side,
Seeking those hands from the other side.
The journey of life is full of mishaps,
But it needs courage to make a new beginning.
Each day is a struggle, each day a strain.
Each morning brings pleasure, each morning brings pain.
Amidst the responsibilities do we forget to live?
Among the challenges do we keep aside the love?
I seek your answer my muted love,
The pain in my heart is heavy.

Can we plan to share some moments of peace?
Some fragments of our shattered parts?
A broken glass is difficult to join.
So leave aside the glass like lives that prick and pain.
Some moments of joy, some feeling of laughter,
With heads on each other's shoulders,
Leaving the world to think its thoughts.

We spend some time hand in hand
In our own strange land.

12
My Child, I Dream With Thee

My love you are in slumber deep,
Being transposed into a world of dreams.
I loved to see you in that peaceful sleep,
My being carried me to years agone,
When you slept carefree in my lap.

I cheered those infant smiles and cries,
Your pulling my hair, your childish plays,
Those small fingers holding my hands,
Are still the same with the passing time,
Only that you grow in mind and matter,
Those blissful moments I now try to gather.

With you beside you I cherish my dreams,
Two pair of eyes dreaming the same dream.
I become your mirror, you see your childhood,
Through the eyes of your mother,
Walking hand in hand, by the beautiful sunny land.

13
My Eyes in Tears

Was it a fault?
My eyes in tears.
Was it a longing?
To be in love.
Was it a thought?
To be his dream.
Was it a passion?
To be his own.
Is this the reality?
To be left alone.

Is this the return?
Years of isolation.
Is this the responsibility?
Over domination.
Is this the care?
Your magnified egoism.
Is this the love?
Your suspicious nature.

I seek my answers in the journey of my life,
That took major turns for your useless strife.

14
My Love Enjoys Being Loved

My love I profess, day in and day out,
My sweetheart hears it all, day in and day out.
His replies I seek, silent lies he,
He is in his own world.
Little afraid, little curious,
Afraid of the strange ways of the world,
He counts me one amongst them.
Fears he to share his love with me,
No longer he seeks commitment.

Who will tell this crazy man,
Life holds something more than liabilities.
He has some hidden fears and pain,
He loves them as his siblings.
His relation with them is strong enough,
Making my professed love a trifling.
My reply he gives with smiles and roses,
After the long letters I write,
This leaves me in a crazed state about my enterprise.

His keenness I admire, his sharp observance,
To be with me when I'm in deep slumber.
Seeing me lost in sleep, he happily replies my letters.
My love do not be proud of being loved so well,
In such a silent way.
Don't absorb my love as a blotting paper.
Rather reflect it back like merry light in distant ways.

15
My Sister in the Journey of My Life

My love, my pride, my sister, my delight.
Memories flash of you as my tender teacher and guide.
Me crying those baby cries to see you go as a bride.
Waiting each year to see my sister,
Seeking permission for her own home.
Happily she came spreading cheer around,
Mother's pride and father's love she adorned.

In my delicate youth she dressed me as a red bride,
Waving me with tearful eyes.
Then began another phase of life,
My sister became my guiding light.
Encouraging me at every step, bearing my fears alone.
She knew my reasons, gave them her voice,
Pulling me out of the dooms.

Her blessings I sought, at times she said,
'I know you will rise very high.'
Her dreams for me made me a bird,
Gave me the wings to fly.
In those flooded times, I became a boatman,
She became my oar taking me to the river's other side.

The journey grew with us together,
Hearing each other's sighs.
She consoled me, I cajoled her
Smiling those infant smiles.
At times I teased her, 'Stop being so young,
It's better you look like a mom'.
My darling dear I want you near,
In all walks of my life.

16
My Students in Pandemic

These naughty ones, those introverts,
All become muzzle headed and the corona they curse.
These pretty souls who longed for vacation,
Seem tired of this long isolation.
Fed up they were of seeing the institutional buildings.
Now they long to see those structures as great treasures.
Those shady trees below which girls had their secret chats.
Those lush green playgrounds where boys showed their flairs.
They miss becoming the last benchers and being the teachers' pet
The eyes of their teachers had rested on them,
Lest they ended up doing something great.
Where's the fun in taking the lunch alone even if there are variations,
The joy that existed in stealing the favourite food
From the backpacks of their friends.

In our online classes they tell me, 'Ma'am show us our classroom'
With eager and sad eyes, as if life's snatched away from them.
Through the isolation that seems immobile.
Everything and every person deem fitting in their position,
The teachers in school without their students,
Are like parents without children.
School is their second home,
I wish time runs by quickly,
And let my kids return to their school
With love for learning in their eyes.

17
Ornamental Love

Oh my love, what is the charm in beautifying my long hair,
When you are not near to take an aroma of them?

What is the essence in creating charm
In my solemn eyes with the thick black liners,
When you are not near to look deep into these eyes?

Why must I wear these diamond studded earrings,
When you don't whisper your love into my ears?

Why do I wear these rainbow coloured bangles,
When you don't hold my hands to take me for long walks?

Why do I adorn my slender legs with these silver anklets,
When you are not near to hear my chiming calls?

For whom do I wear this flowing red saree,
When you don't hold it from behind to give me a pause?

Why do I wear this golden waistband around my belly
When you don't pull me back never to let me go?

18
Let's Get Drenched in the Rain

The rain showers begin
With a low moaning sound,
Seeing the showers fall slow,
My eyes meet your eyes deep.
The showers gain force,
Our heartbeats are on the rise.
My fingers reach out to your hands,
In silence I drag you to the terrace top.

Let us get drenched in the rains my love,
To feel the charm of our youthful love.
Let us hold each other in our arms,
For an eternal journey together.

19
Friends Forever

One of the strangest relations,
Not bound by blood, but by devotion.
This journey has not been too long,
But the beauty it possesses envies others for long.

It began very slow,
Like a seedling into a plant,
It consumed our time and trust,
As nutrition for its body parts.
Both of us were very vigilant,
Before sharing our moments,
Lest time and humans do conspire,
Causing our pleasures to become pain.

We stole time to meet each other,
And still do the same,
Laughing out our pleasures,
Laughing at our pains.
Not a day passes by my friend,
Without a thought of you.
At times you become my mentor,
Other times I guide you.
Years I seek to pass by,
In this beautiful companionship.
Not a day my love wastes by,
In thoughts without you.

20
Friendly Love, Lovely Friend

Two strangers met,
The meeting grew,
It grew in intensity.
Time flew out of hands.

Two strangers meet,
After seven years like strangers again.
The meeting turned to friendship,
The friendship turned to love,
They knew not of it,
When they knew it became too late.
The man said, 'If there can't be love,
Let there be friendship.'
'I'll find love in your friendship,
You find friendship in my love.'

21
A Thousand Reasons for a Reasonless Love

My loving you has reasons less for the world,
Reasons more for me.
It's me who has fallen in love, not this world.
It's me who wait for your moments, not the restless world.
It's me who wish to hear you, not the deaf world.
It's my eyes that search for you,
Not the eagle-eyed world.
It's me longing for your companionship,
Not the fickle world.
My love holds reasons more for you,
The world appears to me a stranger.
My emotions, my inner self try to wrap around you calmly.
With closing eyes I rest against your pounding heart.
This grasp of yours is heavenly.
I don't want to leave this heaven of mine,
For any treasure of this world.

My love I wish the world comes to a standstill,
For you to feel this love of mine.
My sensuality becomes your eagerness,
My smile becomes your strength.
My closeness becomes the aroma of your life,
My receding becomes your pain.
But my love you know not to make me dance in joy,
With your proud and honest love.
Years may pass as thus,
You being silent, I being still,
But for whom to solve this riddle?

22
The Search Continues

O pause the rushing blue sea waves,
I'm waiting for my love.
Searching for him in the bed of red roses,
Hearing him in the rustling yellow leaves,
Fragrancing him in the rain wet mud,
Feeling his touch in the small dew drops.

My love, my senses all call you,
Disagreeing with your hard day's chores.
You be lost in my soft love,
I, in your strong care.
The world aside we keep,
It is time the world is of two.
With your soft look, my heart melts,
In your tender arms I lie,
You find heaven in my long black locks,
I, in the protected shelter of yours.
Ages I seek to pass as thus,
With no grudges, no lies.

As the day takes its leave,
And comes home my love,
I'm for him, he is for me
No cares, no worries,
My love don't keep me in vain,
I'm waiting for the clock to strike,
To hear your footsteps nearing me.
To feel your sensual love.
O night you give him to me
When else do I feel his love?

23
We Meet in Dreams

The morning begins,
The sunlight peeps in, the cool breeze blows.
It reaches the body, stirs the senses.
The eyes open softly, with me holding the pillow,
Reminiscing my encounters with you,
In my picture-perfect dreams.

The world aside in its own chores,
Leaving us alone to be our own
In our world of love.
With none to question, I have none to serve.

These delicate moments I clutch in my grasp,
And pen them into verse.
Oh! The eyes feel drowsy again,
Let me take a leave,
For my love is waiting in my silent dream.
I can't leave him for long,
For his eyes too wait eagerly,
To see me in my charms.

24
When Beauty Meets Body

Wherever we go, a common question,
Do you diet, do you exercise?
Do you know that you are a body?

Years pass by in beautifying the body,
As one thinks another to be a body, which is good indeed.
But do people ever think to look beyond that body?

Beyond that fair skin and beyond that dull hue,
There might be someone intricated with years of complexities.
Am I really beautiful?
Shall I ever be charming?
Years pass by and even a lifetime in this turmoil.
Physical charms captivate, but what about the being?
The soul merges itself so much with the body,
That it forgets its difference from the body.
The eternal thinks itself to be perishable,
Acceptance is received,
Love flows in seeing a flowing figure, a handsome physique.

Do we ever turn to remove the coating of silver,
To know the true nature of the base metal?
Lets' be realistic, life shall turn optimistic.

25
Don't Make Me Fall in Love

Stranger,
Don't make me fall in love,
You step into my world like a shadow,
A shadow that followed me for years,
Then one day the shadow became one with me.

Stranger,
Don't make me fall in love,
Don't look at me so that I get attracted,
Don't talk to me so that I am swayed,
Don't appreciate me so that I look for appreciation
everywhere.
Don't like me so that I think it to be love.

Stranger,
Go back to your world,
And leave me in my world,
As our two worlds are not same.
I'll love you from my world,
You love me from your world.
Stranger, don't make me fall in love.

26
Life's Second Phase

I, sitting by the river bank,
Throwing pebbles in the silent water.
With each drop the water rippled,
With it rippled my thoughts.
I, journeying between my past and present,
In a dilemma to seek the truth.

Thinking over I felt,
Oh, I have begun my life's second phase.
The second phase is promising,
With you by my side.
My strength become you, your care become I.
Your silence I love, my beauty becomes your lifeline.
Years I had spent in search of you,
God saw my tireless walks.
He being the Creator knows the blend of beings,
He stopped me and changed my path.
I walked through the darkness,
Jostling for the light of life.
It was then that I met you,
Welcoming the calmest moments of my life.

My love I plead you be with me,
In the journey of my life.
The world I care least how it thinks,
As I found none to dry my tears.
These caring hands I don't want to leave,
For the folly of the foolish world.

Thinking thus I saw my empty hands,
The pebbles I had, had jumped merrily into the water,
Those empty hands were empty again,
My heart echoed my wish to you,

The hollow echoes returned to me.

I looked up at the sky,
Speaking to God my Father.
My fate you created, my fate you entangled,
My fate I leave to you,
My trust on you is your fate,
Your destiny too now I handle.

27
Love and Art

My love I attained after years of futile search,
My mind wasn't clear about the concept of love.
Did it mean to care for one with conditions?
Did it mean to get a seeking attention?
Was it the fulfillment of roles?
Was it the sharing of responsibilities?
Or was its essence being happy in each other's company?
Without any reason?
Without any turmoil?
Without any distraction?

What was the love I was searching for?
I asked around, no one knew.
I searched around, no one presumed.
I gave in to art.
I found my true love in it.
I knew not that unless revealed,
By an artist true, who said,
'Submergence in art is love in its most unalloyed form.'
The search futile became a dream come true.
Art joins hand with the artist.
For two loves to be united into one true.

28
Loving Through Verses

Two beings met as strangers true,
Bearing none in common between the two,
No topics to touch, no words to relate
No feelings to reciprocate.

Suddenly the woman emerged with some broken verses,
The man found a speck of glow,
Some feelings lay in those uncharmed lays,
A jeweller he was, he knew the ways,
To polish a diamond to its best shape.
He slowly conversed, he slowly read,
The verses she wrote in his silent days.

Thence dawned a day when all on a sudden,
Thus spake he to her: 'Work on your art,
It needs some space.
Free up your emotions cluttered in muddles,
Feel free to express your soul in verses.
Don't you know that's your passion?'
Then began a journey as if into space,
The woman surrendering to her quill's pace.
She wrote and wrote,
He read and read,
He polished her skills in his insane daze.
He never gave her subjects,
Though she asked for them,
He said, 'Think for yourself, God has given you enough brains;
Sift the seeds from the weeds until it rains'.
He became a light in the darkness of the night,
She followed him like shadow,
Never to leave his sight.

Thus began a journey through love for verses,
Its purity surpassed even the blessings of sages.

29
My Lost Love

My love, how is the joy of the pain?
How are the moments of loneliness?
With me there was solitude in joy,
Alone, there is joy in solitude.
Years passed in each other's clasp,
Clinging for spurs of peace.
Fulfilling each other through broken promises of love and
liabilities.

Tell me my love, did I lag behind in roles
To be punished in such severe ways?
There were smiles, there were tears,
Why my love you questioned my space
Leaving no space for me to breathe?
I stepped out of home to breathe my life,
And the breathing continues.

Looking behind I see a house,
Without the joys of a child.
Without the woman asserting her rights,
The house seems no more a home.
No aroma of food, no demands from the child,
No woman her fragrance spreads.

My eyes fill with tears to see such a fear,
The truth of it is bitter.
But life goes on in such a shattered way,
My love how can you be my love anymore?

The relation being dry like the yellow autumn leaves,
Waiting for the tree to be wry.
Spare me my lost love,
This much for this life would suffice.

30
Silence in Grasp

Life had its own pace,
Trodding its own little path, carefree and lone,
The one leading that life felt,
Lone life was her own.

Years passed by, she like a pearl in an oyster shell,
Submerged in her world, like a mind lost in thoughts.
Making no futile searches, for a companionship of ages.
Life dragged on, no one messed on.
Sudden, a change came, slow but with no name.

God sent her a blessing, a reason to smile,
Her loneliness was heard of,
In the silent darkness of the night.
A care so caring, a joy so joyful.
A love so loving, a bliss so blissful.
The vacuum of life was filled,
With eternal trust and strength.
Something she searched to pacify her being.

Few moments of silence, few words of care,
With reception of this all, her life changed for rare.
Fleeting moments she tried to hold fast,
Like a soul trying to reach heaven,
Breaking past the Earth's gravitating grasp.

31
Strangers in Love

Strangers in love,
Couples stay with one another,
Fulfilling each other's responsibilities.

A dryness comes with the lack of romance.
Love asks its space,
Questions its identity.
Slowly it recedes like a frightened animal.
Hiding here and there,
Sometimes even coming to the forefront,
Altogether changed in its form
Questioning no more and no less.

32
Toxic Companionship

An unfailing companionship was thought of,
In its most blooming stage,
When the shy bride sat near the sacred fire,
Swearing the seven vows of marriage.
A proud face her partner owned,
Reflecting the superiority of his class.
With eyes resting on the ground, the bride
Revealed the coyness of her part.

The marriage began with youthful promises,
Dreams big but none to keep governance.
With passing years the relation began to suffocate,
Thus searching for various outlets of escape.
The bride being trapped in a maze of never-ending reasons,
As if her decisions bore no perfection.
Her story bearing the pain, needed listening,
Her heart alone was testimonial of her being forlorn.
Jostling with thousands of fair chances,
Her cluttered little head searched for conclusions.

Where minds don't match, nor do your reasons,
Even you find missing the respect for the relation,
When such stage is reached, love becomes toxic.
It demands removal,
Like a wounded arm being ripped off the body.

The marriage vows that began with such vigour,
Drags on to its finishing line,
Thus opening a world that stings with questions,
Seeking honeyed answers.
All the bride needs now is to feel free as air,
Breaking the chains of iron thus she says,
'My being wants to taste the better side of life,
I want to take leave from you, my toxic married life'.

33
Poisoned Love

My life I began with love in my eyes,
In those early years of youth.
With sheer delicacy, my mind could sustain, my body could
hold.
Falling in love with veiled poison,
Slowly consuming it, nurturing it,
Multiplying it, magnifying it.
Until it began to loosen me, intoxicate me.
I relished the poisoned love.
My senses became numb, darkness spread around,
Closing the world before me,
Showing me the way to another world,
My whole-hearted gratitude to my poisoned love.

34
Mourning Becomes the Festival

The Festival, a source of joy to all,
For her is the storehouse of pain.
Memories lying as dormant seeds,
Get watered by the tears of pain
Her home she left behind,
That she had nurtured with love and liabilities,
Lies in a dead silence without her,
No sound of the chiming anklets,
No air of love and romance,
No cause for celebration,
No joy of the festival season.
Her laughing child spread her laughter,
Wherever she went,
Inwardly she hid her tears,
That only her mother knew.

The pain of separation had weakened her within,
Mother on one bank, father on the other,
A river like distance with the banks promising never to meet
again.
The child was the rope,
Parents were the two ends,
At tugs of war with each other.
The rope finally lost its grip,
Falling to the other side.
One was thus entrusted with love and responsibility,
For a lifetime to keep.

35
Missing Knows No End

Her imaginations they were,
They took her for long walks,
Into the intricate arrays of her mind,
A pattern of connected thoughts.

Feeling the cold water,
Her palm welcoming the reach.
While stood she silently,
Dressing herself as the sensual night queen
Her eyes closed a moment,
Sensing a feel of love.

She stood transfixed,
Lost in her romance,
Her lover giving her his most perfect glance.
O what a shyness she felt,
What a suddenness of passion.
Wrapped in the arms of her lover,
She touched the peak of all emotions.

Eyes opening slowly with hidden smiles,
Her hands drenched in water,
Resuming to normal life.
The night's beauty eagerly awaited her lover,
To trap him in her wily charm.

36
The Shielding Thorn

The beautiful rose asks her gardener slight,
'How do you feel if I shed this thorn of mine?'
With a lovely gesture the gardener prompts,
'This thorn shall protect you my rose,
From the world's evil eyes.'
The rose replies with a burning plight,
'The thorn bleeds me deeply inside,
I cannot bear this recurring pain, my nurturer, my second life.'

The gardener cries with teardrops and sighs,
'How do I leave you unprotected my rose,
Without the thorn in your life?'
'It suffocates me my father killing my zest for life.'
Saying thus the beautiful rose sighs.

With a saddened smile the gardener cuts apart the thorn,
The rose smiled within, she cried within,
On parting from the thorn of her life.

37
Umbilical Bond

The bond between us made by the Almighty great,
Even He does not dare to question it straight.
I grew with you, you grew with me.
Me hopping into youth, you strolling into age.

My mentor you were, when I a child,
Your advisor became I, with the years flowing by.
You shielded me as a silkworm in a cocoon,
Slowly releasing me as a river into sea.
Making me resistant like an iron to a hammer,
To counter intense pain,
Like a weak flower to heavy showers.
Giving me life's great lessons as my supermodel.
Jostling with father to prize me with my rights,
I always beheld you my mother with hopeful eyes.

You listen to me as an angel treading from the sky.
You serve me with your tender hands after hard I toil.
At times twisting my ears saying
'I know you don't like to eat bread.'

Home is homely when mother is around,
Her absence is felt like a king without a crown.
My eyes drain my mother to see you in intense pain,
In the sunset of your life, I hold your hands.
I won't let you take leave my mother,
To go to stranger lands.

38
The Art of Chasing Love

My waiting for you knows no end,
Sunrise to sunshine, sunshine to sunset,
To hear those silent unheard thoughts,
To feel those deep fears of yours,
Of losing me to another world.
To sense that touch of belongingness of yours,
To be that lone star you look at transfixed.

Oh my! My senses are sensed, my feelings are felt.
You near me, a foot ahead each day.
Breathing my thoughts through my poetry deep.
We chase into another world where,
Love becomes art, art becomes love,
Changing forms but being the same.
Artist survives the art, art survives the artist.

39
The Alchemy of Masculine Love

The man dominates upon his woman,
Giving it the name of love.
He subjugates his partner,
Giving it the name of understanding.
He makes her think only in his perspective,
Giving it the name of understanding.
He satiates his lust,
In the name of becoming one.

It is a world more of man,
Where the woman stands happy and alone,
Searching for her identity in him.
Where the woman smiles that artificial smile,
Being caught in a snare laid by him.

40
When Shall the Anklets Chime Again?

The times since time gave me wings,
To feel my body, to feel my being,
I fell in love with anklets bright,
With different hues, with distant chimes.
Creating in me the love for the one,
Of whom I dreamt in my dreams alone.
She came near me in those jingling chimes,
Hearing her my senses came alive.
Then would I see the woman of my dreams,
Sitting close by me in her delicate youth,
With silent love in her eyes.

I would steal near her to hold her tight,
I silently closed my eyes to kiss her light.
When my sensual love reached its zenith,
My craving eyes opened,
With a pressing pillow by my side.
I smiled to myself, I shied within,
My mind still in quest for the woman of my dream.

41
Meandering Love

Each moment was passing,
I was in search of my love.
The search continued,
Like a quest for diamond among coals,
Like a quest for calmness among chaos.

I gave my search a pause,
Are you my passion?
Are you my love?
Are you my heart's desire?
A silent answer came from you,
Yes, my love, your search needs a pause.

Life flows by as a river,
Meandering in search of the unknown.
Unknown even I'm of my love for you,
Both seem to walk the same paths.
Let's sit together, let's think over it.
Are you the love of my life?
Having felt so, having known so,
Let's move on our own paths.
For love is not bound by territories,
Nor is it by space.
It's the heart that nurtures it,
It's the heart that gives it a space.
To breathe permanence as the breathing life,
To let it grow at its pace.

42
Pandemic Love

My love for you has become diseased,
It finds no cure.
Months together have passed this way,
It finds no outlet,
It finds no door.

I, wandering aimless after years of toil,
To keep alive a dying relation,
As if sheltering a flickering light.
My life you resemble the pandemic,
Me alone fighting against your tides.
This emotional fight with the self continues,
The hope within suffocated as a caged bird,
Flaps its wings to fly,
Attempting to soar high in the blue sky.

My love I had cried to be one with you,
To patch up our shattered parts.
Finding you diseased,
I thought to get rid of my infected parts.

My love I equate you to the pandemic,
Waiting to be healed,
Waiting to be cured,
Struggling to shed away your toxic parts.

Soon the world will cleanse itself of the pandemic,
My heart too will liberate itself of its agonizing parts.

43
Futile Search

Spare me, let me live.
You made me a nomad,
Now you want me to be consistent as the sea?
You made me a lunatic in love,
Now when I'm emancipated of this insanity,
You want me to be elitist as a work of art?

Tired of my pursuits you left me free,
Now that I enjoy this freedom,
How can you get back the 'me'?
My lips would call your name endlessly,
Your ears were weary of hearing me,
To give rest to yourself, you thoughtlessly liberated me.
Now your search for me has become as of,
White pearls from the oysters of the sea?

You gave me the time, saying, 'Go, heal yourself, '
The healing continued for years,
Now that the wounds are healed,
You want me to reveal the flesh and blood
That once lured the wandering flies and bees?

You spared me the time,
That duration exceeded,
I'm changed to a person,
Now with hopes and with wings.
Don't attempt now to spread your nets,
For you may get entangled and I may flee.

44
Happiness Unfound

Life moves on in an aimless way as a wanderer,
Searching for something it knows not.
There's a vacuum within, a space lying vacant,
I'm trying to fill it up.

The morning rays fall on my eyes,
Urging me to begin my search.
I look around at people and things,
Seeking comfort in the unknown.

Eyes fall from person to person,
Do you wish to know me?
Seeing them involved in their chores,
Eyes fall on the mirror,
To look at the reflection of 'me'.
The 'me' within can't run away from itself.
It can't stop its thinking.
Asking myself, 'Am I so complex,
For others to give a second thinking?'

Finding solace in the smiling faces, I thought,
It needs not much to be happy at,
Except those small joys of life.
Happiness big doesn't come every day,
We lose scope to smile out our lives.
The small shades of life shade us with love,
Against the tides of our lives.

****